Simple Cooking For Single Dads

(And other **Hungry** Kitchen Chickens)

by:
Lui Campos

AuthorHouse™
1663 Liberty Drive
Bloomington, IN 47403
www.authorhouse.com
Phone: 1-800-839-8640

© 2012 by Lui Campos. All rights reserved.

No part of this book may be reproduced, stored in a retrieval system, or transmitted by any means without the written permission of the author.

Published by AuthorHouse 11/21/2012

ISBN: 978-1-4772-8507-7 (sc)
ISBN: 978-1-4772-8506-0 (e)

Library of Congress Control Number: 2012920484

Any people depicted in stock imagery provided by Thinkstock are models, and such images are being used for illustrative purposes only.
Certain stock imagery © Thinkstock.

Because of the dynamic nature of the Internet, any web addresses or links contained in this book may have changed since publication and may no longer be valid. The views expressed in this work are solely those of the author and do not necessarily reflect the views of the publisher, and the publisher hereby disclaims any responsibility for them.

Cover designed and illustrated
by

Roland Parker

Interior design and illustrations
by

Lacye Beauregard

Table of Contents

Introduction	1
Shopping Lists	4
Condiments	6
Seasoning	7
Slicing, Dicing, Peeling, etc.	8
Cook's Tools	9
Basic Terms	13
Approved Cheating	14
Abbreviations	16

7 Soul Steak	17
Baked Chicken Thighs*	18
Basic Gumbo	19
Beef Stew	20
Beef Stroganoff	21
Bistec Colombiano	22
Butter Potatoes	23
Chicken Soup*	24
Chili	25
Baked Chicken Thighs	26
Steamed Potatoes and Fish	27
Jambalaya	28
Macaroni and Cheese	29
Mashed Potatoes	30
Mashed Sweet Potatoes	31
Meat Sauce with Pasta	32
Meatloaf*	33
Pasta	34
Red Beans	35
Rice	36
Roast Chicken	37
Beef Vegetable Soup	39
About the Author	41

Introduction

Some years ago, I discovered that my two daughters and I were not necessarily doomed to lives of canned soup, frozen pizzas and endless bowls of Ramen Noodles just because I had suddenly become a single dad!

I had always liked good ole'-fashioned home cooking, had learned how to cook some dishes as a bachelor and decided to try my hand at cooking again... *for survival*!

As a psychotherapist with evening appointments in my practice, I did not relish the thought of coming home to cook dinners from scratch late at night. My daughters were eleven and seven at the time. Their "cooking repertoire" consisted of pouring milk over cereal, P & J sandwiches and pulling snacks out of the cookie jar.

I began our experiment by cooking on Sunday afternoons after we came home from church. There were the basics: spaghetti, jambalaya, gumbo (from a package), and beef stew. I would make two main dishes and two vegetables. These I stored in the refrigerator. On week night evenings we pulled out what we wanted for dinner, zapped it in the microwave and served a hot, nutritious and pretty tasty dinner if I do say so myself.. and, I do. More importantly, so did my (finicky/ picky) daughters!

The hassle of starting from scratch every Sunday led to writing down "directions" for each dish. I wrote them down on little pieces of paper which I kept in a toy combination safe... don't ask; it was just handy!

So, tell me if I'm wrong: for the kitchen-challenged, (a.k.a., **Kitchen Chicken**), the stumbling blocks are
    a. "Where do I start? and,
    b. What is step two??"

I decided that, if I could read directions, I would not have to stop and organize my thoughts, as well as my materials and supplies every time I cooked. Besides, the girls kept coming in and out of the kitchen, interrupting me with life threatening issues and questions, such as:

"I have a project due tomorrow and we have to go to the store right now...!"
"Daddy, where are my school clothes..." And, of course, the inevitable,
"Daddy, she won't get out of my room!!....."

Do you know this drill, you single dads out there? So the question is, if you happen not to be a ready-made cook, how do you juggle both sets of demands?

This little book is designed with you in mind if...

a. You are not sure what all those little buttons are for on that thing they call a stove,
b. You have never peeled a potato or chopped an onion,
c. Stew, meatloaf, and 7-Soul Steak are things you've eaten, but never considered that they were all raw at one time and did not grow in a stew or meatloaf garden some where...
d. You are afraid of the concepts described in a., b. and c., and/or,
e. In other words, YOU ARE a KITCHEN CHICKEN!

What you will learn is **HOW TO**
- Shop for the necessary food items
- Organize a set of basic cook's tools
- And, how to cook basic, tasty home-cooked meals

Yes, I mean you who thought that sauté was what you say when you thrust a sword in a sword fight! (Did you even know how to spell it....No? well, first lesson: Now you do!!)

AN INTERESTING SIDE EFFECT

When my little pieces of paper with cooking directions had accumulated to the point that they started falling out of the little safe I had been stuffing them into, I decided it was time to get a notebook. After about 10 different dishes were written (which has grown to over 30 and counting) it occurred to us that we needed to name this process of Sunday cooking together. We wrote down several names, voted and thus was born The Measuring Spoon Café*... ta daah!

By this time, Sunday afternoons had become a time for my daughters and me to be together, cook together and catch-up on the comings and goings of the week. That's right, my 11 and 7 year old and I formed an assembly line around the cooking counter. There were vegetables to peel and scrub, AND dice and slice. Eventually, there were pots to stir and condiments to add and "taste test". Ultimately, in time, the girls each tried their hand at some of the basic dishes...

Not a bad way to find time to talk, teach, laugh and learn, no? If you are interested,
read on, and enjoy!

During the writing of this book, the LOGO* has taken on a larger meaning for me. Because I remember the young years of my daughters in connection to these dishes I believe I will take a writer's prerogative and add this recipe:

HOW TO MEASURE OUT SPOONFULS OF A FATHER'S INGREDIENTS –
1 Tbs each of sweetness, affection and praise
2 Tbs of discipline
3 Tbs Positive Role Modeling

A special ingredient

How to get delicious meals:

1. Until you get the hang of it, follow the directions.
2. Taste and Taste and Taste… make your dishes taste scrumptious.
3. Stay in the kitchen; watch over your dish; use a timer.
4. Don't burn stuff, and
5. Put love into your cooking, so you'll love what you've cooked.

Shopping Lists

If you have been to the grocery store and bought seasoning, vegetables and meats SKIP THIS SECTION, GO STRAIGHT TO THE RECIPES

If you are truly a novice, (or a Kitchen Chicken), here is a descriptive shopping list of items that you can use as a reference when preparing the dishes in this book.

Generally, each direction/recipe will list the ingredients you will need for each dish.

FOOD ITEMS

I. **Chicken** – Poultry Section of the Grocery Store
   1. Whole chicken, labeled "Fryer" or "Young Chicken". Steer away from chicken labeled "Hen"
   2. For Gumbo or Jambalaya, get boneless/skinless thighs
   3. For Baked Leg Quarters, look for packs that have the drumstick and thigh still connected; usually labeled "leg quarters". For this dish you can also simply buy "thighs".

II. **Beef**
   1. For Stew:
      a. Most stores have pre-cut packs labeled "stew meat". This is generally fine. These packs use a cheaper cut and this can mean the meat will be a bit tougher than the better cuts. It is still tasty…
      b. However, as one butcher told me, "As long as you boil it long enough, it will get tender. Heck! You could boil an old pair of boots and if you do it long enough they'll come out tender!!" Remember that.
      c. If you want to do "fancy", get a Rump Roast or Sirloin and cut it down to bite size cuts.
      d. Any other cut of meat in between these two boiled alone for an hour should cook down tender enough.
   2. For Meat Sauce (with Pasta Dishes) in my order of preference for low fat/best flavor (Most expensive to cheapest – in most stores)
      a. ground sirloin
      b. ground beef
      c. ground chuck

(Beef, Cont'd)
3. 7- Steak: Ask the butcher/meat attendant for assistance; this cut may only be available in certain stores. You can use round steak as a substitute.
4. Roast
   a. Bottom roast
   b. Chuck roast

III. Sausage
1. Pork Sausage (Hickory smoked is very tasty)
2. Pork/beef combination (a little less fat)Turkey Sausage (Smoked and made to taste like pork: HEALTHIER)
3. Anduille (for gumbo only)

IV. Pork
1. For simple Roast Pork, get a Sirloin Roast, boneless, or
2. Picnic Roast, this one will cook "fork tender"
3. Pork chops (for frying)

V. Veggies
1. **Fresh**
   Potatoes: White Russet Potatoes, 5 lb. bag (there are others you can try)
   Carrots… Pack of about 10
   Celery… comes in a "bunch"
   Green Onions… come in a "bunch"
   White Onions, Yellow Onions, Purple Onions… buy them singly (Though some are sold in bags of 6 or 8, I would recommend singly at first. If you find you like slicing and chopping, then get the bag.)
2. **Frozen Vegetables**
   You will need to experiment to see which veggies will suit the palates you are cooking for, especially if you are a single dad cooking for picky eaters. Generally, the usual vegetables you will need are
   a. Lima Beans (baby limas or regular limas)
   b. Kernel Corn (or corn on the cob)
   c. Green Beans
   d. Mixed Vegetables
   e. Broccoli
   f. Black Eyed Peas
   g. Butter Beans
   h. Peas
   i. Yellow Squash
   j. Zucchini
   k. Spinach

VI. STAPLES (things to always have around)

1. Rice – White rice, long grain
2. Beans – Best if bought in dry form Red Beans (aka kidney beans), Great Northern or Navy Beans, White Lima Beans
3. Pasta – Each pasta dish will call for a specific pasta. The directions will say which one. Here are some examples: spaghetti, linguini, rotinni, and ziti (pick pasta by name).
4. Tomato Sauce – 8 oz. can. Keep two or three in your pantry all the time.
5. Rotel (brand) This is a tomato and chili combination, sometimes sold as generic; used to add spice to a number of dishes. I usually use the "Original" which is spicy enough. You will need to experiment. There is "mild", "original", and "hot"; also, "Original" and "Chunky" (that sort of depends on whether you like tomatoes)
6. Packaged Bread Crumbs – These come in different flavors. Start with basic, and let your taste buds guide you to other flavors.

VII. CONDIMENTS/SPICES

This aspect of cooking can get complicated by personal tastes, especially if you are trying to satisfy finicky eaters. The best approach is to start with the basics and add-in small increments that taste good to you and the ones for whom you are cooking. That is what is meant "to taste". Or, you can do what I did: I introduced my girls to what I thought was good AND, they adjusted. I was fortunate because they were not too finicky with regard to spices, and seemed to enjoy the flavors I introduced them to.

1. Bare Bone Basics -- Iodized Salt and Black Pepper.
2. Your List – Fill in the blank with your favorites….
3. My List:
   Throw caution to the wind and try my standard set of spices and condiments. They are the ones I use for the dishes in this book. It's your call, adventure or caution…..
   a. Garlic and Parsley Salt (McCormick makes a good blend; 12 oz.)
   b. Tony Chachere's Original Blend. It contains: salt, red pepper, black pepper, chili powder and garlic. If you cannot find it call them at 800-551-9066.
   c. Garlic Powder (granulated, several brands make an adequate powder;10 oz)
   d. Ground Cumin (2 or 3 oz)

VII. CONDIMENTS/SPICES (CONTINUED)

- e. Chicken Flavored Bouillon (I prefer the powdered form by Knorr); some people prefer the cubes. The powder dissolves more easily. Both are comparable in flavor.
- f. Dried parsley Flakes
- g. Shrimp and Crab Boil (concentrated liquid; by Zatarain's; 8 oz.)
- h. Whole Dry Bay Leaf (Rex makes a nice large 16 oz. jar)
- i. Oregano; used in tomato sauces
- j. Basil, also used with tomato sauce. Grind some pine nuts and mix with ground garlic, basil, grated parmesan cheese and mix with olive oil, and Presto! You have "pesto", which you can mix with pasta (a little goes a long way) when you're feeling adventurous. Be careful, though, kids have been known to mutiny violently if the dish looks weird… then again, green spaghetti might just be the coolest!

VIII. SEASONING

"Chopped Onions, etc."

For most good dishes you will need a mix of about ¾ to 1 cup of the following chopped blend:

- a. 1 white onion, sliced/chopped
- b. 3 garlic cloves, fine chopped
- c. ¼ cup of parsley, fine chopped
- d. 2 stalks of green onions, sliced/chopped, and
- e. ½ bell pepper fine chopped

In the beginning of my cooking experience I chopped and sliced by hand. It is fun to do and to perfect if you have the time…

For busy single dads (or if you are not too much of a perfectionist) I recommend that you find a ready-chopped pack of those ingredients. Many stores sell a 16 oz. pack of the very same ingredients, already chopped for you. This is SUCH a time saver… If you do not find the fresh pack, you might look in the frozen foods for a bag of frozen chopped onions, etc. before resorting to the hand chop method if you want to save time. However, use the frozen "chopped onions, etc." within two cookings; that is, don't let them sit in the freezer beyond two times that you cook, as they will lose their potency. Experiment and decide for yourself.

IX. SLICING DICING AND PEELING

The first order of business in slicing and dicing is the knife. The full set will be discussed in the "tools" section. For now, it will suffice to say that you will need a good, sharp solid "chef's knife" for this task.

Slicing requires a firm grip with the non-dominant hand on the vegetable and a downward/slicing motion with the dominant hand. Each direction/recipe will instruct you about which vegetable needs handling. Following are some illustrations that might help.

Slicing and Dicing

Peeling

With a paring knife

Or with a "potato peeler":

X. COOK'S TOOLS

1. Knives – A good starter's set will contain
   a. A Chef's Knife – It's about 12 inches long, with a curved blade, ending in a sharp tip. The curve facilitates slicing, while keeping a steady hold on your cutting board

   b. A Paring Knife – Same shape, but only 4 to 8 inches long

Somewhere along the way after you decide you are really serious about graduating from Kitchen Chicken to Serious Cook, step up to a complete set. Expect to pay $50.00 to $200.00 or more, for a good set of knives –

COOK'S TOOLS (Continued)

2. Cooking Spoons –

   a. MEASURING SPOONS –The set will include the following measurements: ¼ tsp; ½ tsp; 1 tsp; and 1 Tbs

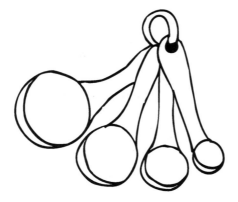

   b. WOODEN SPOONS – For stirring: short and long handle

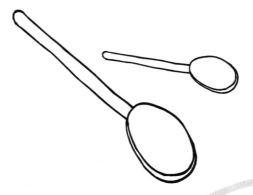

XII. COOK'S TOOLS (continued)

3. Serving Utensils – ladle, serving spoon with holes, potato masher, long fork, spatula, pasta fork

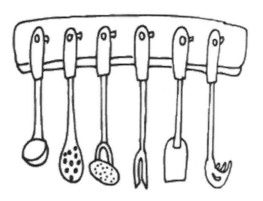

4. Kitchen Timer - For keeping track of time

5. POTS AND PANS – These can be bought in complete sets. If you buy them individually, the basic collection can include at least the following:

   a. A 2-quart saucepan; and a 1-quart saucepan with handle –

   b. A 10-inch and an 8-inch skillet –

   c. A Stock Pot (or Dutch Oven); these come in different sizes. A practical size can be any of these: 5, 6, or 8 quart Stock Pot/ Dutch Oven

6. MIXING BOWLS, MEASURING CUP:

7. COLANDER

8. CUTTING BOARD

9. Baking dish - 9"x 13"x 2"

XIII. BASIC TERMS

1. **Bouillon** – this is a light broth that is obtained by straining the water in which you have boiled chicken or meat. The broth can also be prepared by mixing water with the packaged Bouillion cubes or powder. At any rate it is the liquid that is called BOUILLION.

2. **Brown, or, to brown** – I use this term when preparing certain meats:
   a. Ground beef – Take the required amount (say 1 pound) of thawed ground beef, put it in a skillet or sauce pan, set the flame/burner on "high", with no oil/margerine and with a long wooden spoon keep turning the meat until all the meat turns from red to brown. By constant stirring, you will insure all the meat touches the hot surface AND the ground beef wil turn "crumbley"
   b. Steak or sliced meat – Set the flame/burner on "high" and let the meat sit briefly on one side then with a fork, turn to the other, just long enough to turn it brown.
   c. BROWNING IS DONE JUST PRIOR TO WHATEVER IS THE NEXT STEP IN THE DIRECTIONS

   The idea is to only let the meat turn brown AND THEN Proceed
   d. Drain the liquid fat off the browned meat.

3. **Sauté** – To cook or brown in a pan or skillet in a small amount of butter, oil or both. Usually when I refer to this I am speaking of cooking chopped onions, etc. in a skillet or pan while adding spices. Use a wooden spoon to stir it up; usually cooked for about 3 to 5 minutes. Sauteing is an early step in the process of a dish.

4. **Simmer** – To allow to cook for a specified time, covered, over very low heat. With a gas stove, you should barely be able to see the flame. On an electric stove, set at the lowest setting. Some electric stoves have a "simmer" setting… use it.

5. **Steam** – To cook with very little liquid (usually not more than about ¼ of a cup). The item being steamed is usually a vegetable. Steaming is done for a short time (since there is low liquid). Steaming vegetables leaves them a little firm and preserves their nutrients…. It means we're not cooking until they get soggy or mushy!

6. **Sauce** – A prepared liquid that has a number of ingredients in it (like chopped onions, etc.) to create a paricular flavor; usually poured over as a flavorful addition to the main dish.

7. **Seasoning** – The very heart of a dish: its flavourful essence. It begins with the spices/condiments that suit your palate (and those for whom you are cooking) but includes the add-ons like chopped onions, plus your spices.

8. **Parboil** – Boiling meat (usually) in water for about 15 minutes. This partially cooks it. When the 15 minutes are up (your timer goes ding!), turn off the burner and move the pot to a cool surface (e.g. an unused burner or a trivet)

9. **Trivet** – a small wooden or metal plate (8" or 10") on which to put hot pots

XIV. APPROVED CHEATING

Hey, let us not forget that this is supposed to be a book for simple cooking, that is, EASY! so here are shortcuts that take you a little away from pure cooking but are shorter and simpler than the long way, yet do not sacrifice taste:

1. **Chopped Onions, etc**. – A good, basic sauce contains chopped onions, garlic, green onions, fresh parsley, celery, and bell peppers. Now folks, I started out chopping all of these. It took a LOT of time! If you want to take the time, knock yourself out. There is an approved short-cut. Many stores sell a package of all these (fresh) ingredients already chopped for you. It usually comes in a 16 oz. pack. I have been using this method soon after I started the "Measuring Spoon Café". No one has ever taken away my measuring spoons!

2. **Diced Tomatoes** – Canned tomatoes, diced tomatoes, chopped tomatoes, and pureed tomatoes can be used in a number of the sauces and dishes described in this book. Tomatoes are canned at their prime and may be more flavorfull than store bought tomatoes.

3. **Vegetables** – Most of the vegetables in the dishes in this book can be bought frozen. I will recommend "fresh" in the directions.

4. **Packaged Yellow Rice** (Mahatma makes a very good and easy one)

5. **Packaged Jambalaya or Gumbo Base** -- Oak Grove is a good one; if stores don't carry this in your part of the country, the Oak Grove folks in Prairieville, Louisiana would be glad to ship you some. There's a 12 pack minimum and you can mix, e.g., 6 of Jambalaya, 6 of Gumbo base... Their phone number is (225) 673-6857. Tell 'em I said hello!

6. **Packaged Beef Stroganoff** – McCormick makes a number of ready made mixes for sauces and dishes. These usually call for basic items and "add the package" directions. The "Beef Stroganoff (easy style) is one of these. Just follow the direcitions on the package. If you want more flavor, go to "Beef Stroganoff (more flavor)" in the Directions" section.

7. **Kitchen Bouquet** – This is a bottle of light seasoning and color. It's a quick way to get brown gravy.

8. **Marinara Sauce** – This is a tomato sauce sold already seasoned for use with pasta dishes. It can be plain Marinara or with any number of delicious combinations of added ingredients. This product usually comes in 15 or 17 oz jars. Again, experimentation is the rule of the day. You will find this sauce next to the pasta, with such added ingredients as
    a. Sun-fired tomatoes
    b. Mushroom and onions
    c. Basil and onions
    d. Garlic and onions
    e. And many others that you will HAVE to try to decide

9. **A FINAL WORD ABOUT APPROVED CHEATING**

McCormick's Packaged Seasoning – You would think one of the easiest formulas for failry good dishes is to simply pick out a Packaged Seasoning packet, follow the directions right on the package AND THAT WOULD BE THAT. To some extent I agree and that may very well be all you have to do, especially if you are in a SUPER hurry or your taste buds are fairly easily satisfied. HOWEVER... Don't get carried away!! I have tried a number of these very handy packets. What I have done is used them as a BASIS. Then I add my own touch, and Voila! They taste so much better when you add your own personal touch! So, let's say, Hats off to Mrs. McCormick, and then, let's help her along a little bit and ENJOY le diference'!

Abbreviations

tsp = teaspoon

Tbs = Tablespoon

Cup = cup

lb = pound

oz = ounce

pt = pint

qt = quart

approx = approximately

Dash or pinch = less than 1/8 teaspoon

Dab = about 1 to 2 teaspoops

c. = about/approximately

7 Soul Steak

(NOTE: If you cannot find this cut of meat at your store, get round steak)

YOU WILL NEED
- A 10-inch skillet with a lid
- 1 lb 7 Steak (If you cannot find a 7 steak, get Round Steak)
- 10 oz can of Beef Broth
- ¼ Cup cooking oil OR olive oil
- ½ Cup chopped onions, etc
- 1 tsp Garlic and Parsley Salt

PREPARATION
- Cut the meat into 3 or 4 parts

COOKING
- Pour oil in skillet, heat at "high"
- ADD chopped onions, etc and sauté
- ADD seasoning, mix and sauté for 2 minutes
- Brown each piece of meat about 30 seconds on each side right over the sautéed onions, etc.
- ADD 1 can of beef broth PLUS ½ can of water
- Cook at low heat for 1 hour
- Check every 15 minutes or so; make sure heat setting is not too high, and that the mixture does not dry up (if necessary, add ¼ cu water to keep water at meat level)
- Serve. (GOES WELL WITH BUTTER POTAOES OR RICE, AND A VEGETABLE)
- ENJOY!

Baked Chicken Thighs*

YOU WILL NEED
- 9x13x2 inch baking pan; metal is ok, Pyrex (oven proof) is ideal
- 4 or 6 chicken thighs (1 or 2 per person); can be thigh only or "leg and thigh quarters"
- 1 ½ Cup of chopped onions, etc.
- 1 Tbs Garlic and Parsley Salt (OPTIONAL: 1 tsp of Tony Chachere for spice)
- ½ Cup water
- Aluminum foil

PREPARATION
- Preheat oven to 350 degrees
- Cut off loose fat from the chicken
- Spread 1 Cup of the chopped onions, etc. across the bottom of the pan
- Sprinkle the Garlic and Parsley Salt over the chopped onions, etc.
- Directly from the Garlic and Parsley salt container, lightly sprinkle all over each chicken thigh (plus Tony's if desired)
- Place in the baking dish; they can be touching but make sure each thigh sits separately
- Pour the water around the outer edge of the chicken thighs
- Sprinkle the other ½ Cup of chopped onions, etc. over the thighs
- Cover the pan with a sheet of aluminum foil, curl the edges over the sides of the pan

COOKING
- Place pan in oven and cook for 1 hour
- After they have been cooking for an hour, open the oven and carefully remove the sheet of aluminum foil
- Turn each thigh over, check for tenderness (NOTE: if pink juice seeps out when you puncture any of the thigh meat with a fork OR knife tip, cook 25 additional minutes)
- If there is no pink juice when you check (or after the additional 25 minutes), cook uncovered (skin side up) for 10 to 15 minutes until the meat turns slightly golden
- Take out of the oven, serve and
- ENJOY!

*NOTE: See "Baked Chicken Thighs with Carrots and Potatoes" for additional ingredients

Basic Gumbo

YOU WILL NEED
- 6-qt Dutch Oven
- Colander
- 2 links Anduille Sausage (or Smoked Sausage, see meat section)
- 2 - 3 lb chicken (boneless/skinless chicken thighs)
- ½ Cup frozen okra
- 1 Cup chopped onions, etc.
- 2 tsp Garlic Salt with Parsley (OPTIONAL, FOR SPICE, ½ tsp of Tony Chachere)
- 2 Bay Leaves
- 1 10-oz can of Rotel (OPTIONAL, for spice!)
- 1 15 oz pack of Oak Grove Gumbo Base
- 2 Tbs cooking oil or olive oil
- Dab of margarine
- 2 qt water
- 1 Tbs of chicken bouillon (OR 3 cubes of chicken bouillon)
- 1 Cup of cooked white, long grain rice (see directions for cooking rice)

PREPARATION
- Slice Anduille (or sausage) in ½ inch slices and then re-slice each slice into 2 or 4 pieces
- Cut chicken up into "bite size" chunks
- Parboil the chicken in 2 qts of water with the bouillon for c. 15 minutes
- After boiling the chicken, strain it through the Colander and set the chicken aside, SAVE THE CHICKEN BROTH

COOKING
- Place the oil and the margarine into Dutch Oven, heat at "High" setting
- Sauté the onions, etc. for c. 2 minutes,
- Add the chicken and the sausage, mix and sauté another 2 minutes,
- Add the pack of Oak Grove gumbo Base, stir, ADD Bay Leaves
- Add the frozen okra, stir and mix thoroughly for c. 2 minutes
- ADD can of Rotel (OPTIONAL, for spice!)
- Slowly add the 2 qts of the chicken broth
- Cook over "low heat" setting (bubbling, but not rolling boil) for 40 minutes, covered
- Cook your rice
- Stir gumbo every 10 or 15 minutes, and adjust to taste
- Serve over c. 1/3 Cup of white rice in bowls
- ENJOY

Beef Stew

YOU WILL NEED
- 6-qt Stock Pot (Dutch Oven)
- 1 lb stew beef (or rump roast, see "beef" section), cut to bite size pieces
- 1 Cup chopped onions, etc.
- Slice and dice 4 white potatoes
- 4 carrots (clip off the ends, scrape the skin off with a knife, then slice)
- 1 stalk of celery (snap off of the main stalk, clip off the ends, then slice)
- 1 Cup frozen peas
- 2 tsp Garlic Salt with Parsley (OPTIONAL, ½ tsp Tony Chacher's, for added spice)
- 1/3 cup all purpose flour
- 2 Cups water (for the actual stew)
- 2 Tbs cooking oil
- "dab" of margarine
- Pot of rice (see directions)

PREPARATION
- Measure ingredients; cut up veggies and meat; set aside
- In microwave or on stove, heat 2 Cups of water; don't have to boil. Set aside
- OPTIONAL STEPS (ONLY if you have enough time)
    - (a) Boil the stew beef in about 4 Cups of water with 2 tsp of chicken/beef bouillon; Slow boil (i.e., rolling on medium heat) for 30 to 60 minutes. This will make the meat tender
    - (b) Once you have finished boiling, remove the meat, set it aside and save the broth

COOKING
- Sauté chopped onions, etc. in oil and margarine, with the spices in your 6-qt pot approx 3 – 4 minutes, at "high" setting
- ADD the meat, the potatoes, celery, carrots and peas; continue to sauté; lower setting to "medium"
- ADD the flour. Mix thoroughly. Keep mixture moving for approx 1 minute. It will begin to dry…
- SLOWLY, add Cup #1 of hot water (or the beef broth from the meat). STIR.
- Pour Cup #2 OF THE WATER (or broth); just enough water to be about 1 inch above stew ingredients
- Stir well. Adjust to taste*. Cook covered 30 to 45 minutes (at "low" to "medium"; bubbling, but not rolling boil), stirring every 15 minutes or so
- Make sure there is always water in the stew, about 1 inch above the stew
- While the stew is cooking, PREPARE YOUR RICE
- When all the potatoes, carrots and the meat are thoroughly cooked (potatoes and carrots are easily pierced with a fork; take out a small piece of meat, taste for tenderness) serve over rice
- ENJOY!

* "Adjust to taste" simply means to add spice/salt until it tastes good to you

Beef Stroganoff
(MORE FLAVOR STYLE*)

YOU WILL NEED
- 10-inch skillet with lid or 6-qt Dutch Oven
- 1 long wooden spoon
- A package of McCormick's Beef Stroganoff
- 1 lb of beef (round steak is ok; sirloin is better; and sirloin tip is best)
- IF YOU USE "SIRLOIN TIP" READ THE "NOTE" under "preparations"
- 2 Tbs cooking oil or olive oil
- Dab of margarine
- 8 oz pack of sour cream
- 1 tsp of Garlic Salt with Parsley
- ½ tsp of Tony Chachere
- 1 tsp of beef or chicken bouillon powder (or 1 cube of either)
- ½ white onion
- 1 Cup chopped onions, etc.
- 2 Cups water
- OPTIONAL: ½ Cup sliced mushrooms (white or portabella; you slice them or buy them sliced)
- 1 12-oz pack of EGG NOODLES

PREPARATIONS
- (If using round steak or sirloin) slice up the meat in ½ in wide, 2 inch long strips
- Boil the sliced up pieces of round steak in 2 Cups water with the bullion powder/cubes for 30 minutes
- Drain the meat, set the broth aside
- Slice the half white onion from top to bottom in thin slices then separate all the slices

COOKING
- Pour oil and add dab of butter into skillet; put on "high" setting
- Sauté the chopped onions, etc., the sliced white onions and the mushrooms using a wooden spoon
- Add the seasoning (i.e., the Garlic and Parsley Salt and the Tony Chachere) sauté 3 to 5 minutes
- Add the meat (parboiled round steak) and the McCormick's package; mix thoroughly
- NOTE – If you use sirloin tip, you DO NOT have to boil it. It is a tender cut of meat and will cook well without boiling. At this point, you are adding the Sirloin Tip raw. Sauté until all surfaces of the sliced Sirloin Tip are brown
- Add one Cup of the broth, stir well and cook about 25 to 30 minutes at "LOW HEAT" covered; As soon as you cover the skillet START THE PASTA. NOTE: stir the sauce approx every 10 minutes. Add some of the broth you set aside if necessary to keep the sauce "saucy".
- WHEN THE NOODLES ARE DONE and the sauce has cooked approx 30 minutes......ADD the 8-oz pack of sour cream to meat sauce; mix well; cook about 5 minutes.
- Serve the Stroganoff sauce over your DRAINED noodles:
- ENJOY!

*FOR "EASY STYLE" see "Approved Cheating" under "Packaged Beef Stroganoff"

Bistec Colombiano

(COLOMBIAN STEAK)

YOU WILL NEED
- A 10-inch skillet, with lid
- 1 to 1 ½ lb round steak
- 3 white potatoes
- 1 large tomato
- 1 large white onion
- 2 Tbs vinegar
- 3 tsp Garlic and Parsley Salt
- 2 Tbs oil

PREPARATION
- Season both sides of the meat with 1 tsp of Garlic/Parsley Salt, then cut 1 inch slits on four opposite sides of the meat
- Peel the potatoes, then slice them in ¼ inch slices
- Remove the dry peeling from the onion, cut off the top and bottom, then slice the onion in ¼ inch slices,
- Do the same with the tomato

COOKING
- Place the skillet on a burner and set on high,
- Pour the oil into the skillet and move it around to coat all the bottom of the skillet
- Place the meat on the skillet; brown on both sides
- Cover the steak with a layer of potatoes slices; sprinkle with the Garlic/Parsley Salt
- Then a layer of onions slices, sprinkle with the seasoning
- Then a layer of tomatoes, sprinkle with seasoning,
- Alternate layers of potato slices and tomato slices, seasoning each layer
- Finish with a layer of tomatoes,
- Cover and steam on high heat setting for 5 minutes,
- Then, carefully lift the lid, pour the vinegar around the edges of the skillet,
- Cover again, cook at low heat for approx 25 minutes
- It is ready when the tomatoes and the onions are fully cooked
- Serve,
- ENJOY!

Butter Potatoes

(This can be funny to prepare... and tastes great!)

YOU WILL NEED
- A 2-qt saucepan, with lid
- A long wooden spoon (OPTIONAL)
- Pot Holders (OPTIONAL)
- A large bowl
- 4 – 6 White/Russet potatoes (1 potato per serving)
- 1 tsp of Garlic and Parsley Salt
- ½ tsp salt
- 2 Tbs margarine
- 2 – 4 Cups water, for cooking
- 1 tsp dry parsley flakes

PREPARATION
- Peel the potatoes, and cut in quarters, and set aside in a bowl with enough water to cover the pieces

COOKING
- After you pour the water out of the holding bowl, place the potato pieces in the saucepan, add enough water to cover the potatoes by about one inch, add ½ tsp salt and heat to boil ("high heat" setting) for about 20 minutes; the potatoes are done when you can stick a fork easily into any piece
- When they are done turn the heat OFF, UNTIL YOU ARE READY TO SERVE THEM
- 5 minutes before you serve the potatoes, make sure they are still hot (you can "kick up the heat" JUST UNTIL it boils to make sure they are hot)
- Pour out the liquid, sprinkle the Garlic/Parsley Salt, the parsley flakes and ADD THE BUTTER
- Now, either
  - a. Stir the potatoes with the wooden spoon until the butter is well blended, OR
  - b. (OPTION "b") put the cover on the pot and HOLDING THE LID AND THE POT WITH THE POT HOLDERS SHAKE THE POT ROUND AND ROUND UNTIL THE MOTION MIXES THE BUTTER THROUGHOUT THE POTATOES, (this method can look a bit comical if you shake more than just the pot, and the kids will think you are crazy...)
- When the butter has been thoroughly mixed with the potatoes, sprinkle them with dry parsley flakes (for color)
- Serve
- ENJOY!

Chicken Soup*

YOU WILL NEED
- 6-qt Dutch Oven
- 1 lb chicken (either boneless/skinless thighs OR breast filet)
- 6 to 8 Cup of water
- 3 carrots
- 1 stalk of celery
- 2 white potatoes
- 1 Cup frozen "mixed vegetables" (or more "popular" frozen veggies)
- 2 Tbs cooking oil
- "dab" of margarine
- 1tsp Garlic and Parsley Salt (OPTIONAL: ½ tsp of Tony Chachere's)
- 2 tsp chicken bouillon powder (or 2 cubes), or alternately, 1 can of chicken broth

PREPARATION
- Scrape carrot skin off with sharp edge of knife, cut off ends, then slice into ½ inch slices
- Peel and dice potatoes (Alternately, slice potatoes in lengthwise, ¼ inch slices)
- Cut off ends of celery stalk, then slice
- Slice and dice the chicken (c. ½ inch squares)

COOKING
- Sauté chopped onions etc. in 2 Tbs hot oil,
- ADD seasoning, sauté total of 3, 4 minutes
- ADD chicken, sauté additional 3 minutes, UNTIL chicken has cooked on all sides and mixed thoroughly with onions and seasoning, then
- STEAM mixture covered for about 1 - 2 minutes (i.e., cook at medium heat COVERED)
- Take off lid CAREFULLY (steam might burn you), ADD all vegetables, including frozen vegetables (NOTE: you may substitute other types of frozen veggies)
- STIR AND MIX thoroughly,
- ADD water and bouillon powder/cubes or broth
- Let boil for 5 minutes, ADJUST TO TASTE, then COVER and cook at medium/low heat for 30 minutes
- Serve with ladle into bowls
- ENJOY!

*ALTERANTELY, LEAVE OUT THE POTATOES AND 3 CARROTS, REPLACE WITH ½ CU TWICE BROKEN SPAGHETTI OR 1 CUP EGG NOODLES FOR CHICKEN NOODLE SOUP!

Chili

YOU WILL NEED
- 6-qt Dutch Oven
- 1 lb ground beef (see section on beef)
- 1 12oz can of "chili beans" WITHOUT MEAT
- A wooden spoon
- 1 pack of chili mix (McCormick's)
- 1 cup chopped onions, etc.
- 1 tsp Tony Chachere
- 1 tsp Garlic and Parsley Salt
- 1 8oz can of tomato sauce (can be substituted with 10-oz can of Rotel for extra spice)
- 1 Tbs cooking oil OR olive oil
- Saltine Crackers

PREPARATION
- Brown meat in Dutch Oven over high heat
- Drain the grease (with pot holders, hold the lid with a slight crack to allow grease to drain out. Tilt Dutch Oven as you drain the grease into a container, like a tin can)
- Take the meat out of the pan, once drained, and set it aside

COOKING
- Pour oil in same Dutch Oven and sauté the onions, etc for 2 minutes,
- ADD the Chili Mix, the Tony's and the Garlic and Parsley Salt, stir and sauté
- ADD the meat, mix with wooden spoon
- ADD the tomato sauce (OR Rotel), stir and mix
- ADD the chili beans, including the liquid
- Mix thoroughly , add water if the mixture appears too dry
- Cook covered for 15 minutes,
- Serve in soup bowls with Saltine crackers on the side
- ENJOY

Baked Chicken Thighs

WITH CARROTS AND POTATOES

PROCEED AS WITH "BAKED CHICKEN THIGHS"

YOU WILL ALSO NEED, IN ADDITION
- 4 WHITE Russet potatoes
- 6 carrots
- ¾ Cup water

PREPARATION
- Preheat oven to 350 degrees
- Peel and slice the potatoes into 6 pieces
- Scrape the carrots with a knife edge and slice
- After you have spread the chopped onions, etc. spread the potato and carrot slices across the bottom of pan
- Place the chicken over the sliced potatoes/carrots (you might place a few of the potato/carrot pieces in between the chicken thighs)

COOKING
- Proceed as with "Baked Chicken Thighs"
- Bake for same amount of time
- After ½ hour, carefully uncover the aluminum foil and check the potatoes and carrots

They are done if a knife slides easily into any slice of the potatoes or carrots; MOVE THE POTATOES AND CARROTS AROUND THAT ARE ON THE SURFACE IF THEY ARE HARD.
Re-cover with the foil, and continue as with "Baked Chicken Thighs"

Steamed Potatoes and Fish

YOU WILL NEED
- A 10-inch skillet with lid
- 3 or 4 fish fillets (Tilapia, Catfish or Trout)
- 3 or 4 white potatoes
- 1 large white onion
- 1 large tomato
- 2 tsp Parsley and Garlic Salt (can substitute Lemon and Pepper Salt)
- 1 Tbs oil
- 3 Tbs lemon juice (fresh squeezed preferably)
- OPTIONAL: 1 Tbs of capers

PREPARATION
- Season both sides of the fillets with 1 tsp of the Garlic and Parsley Salt (or the Lemon Pepper Salt)
- Peel and slice the potatoes into ¼ inch slices
- Remove the dry peeling from the onion, cut off the top and bottom, then slice it into ¼ inch slices
- Do the same with the tomato

COOKING
- Place the skillet on the stove and set on high
- Pour the oil into the skillet, move it around to coat the bottom of the skillet
- Place the fillets in the skillet; carefully turn them once. (If you are using capers, cover the first layer of the fillets with the capers; continue)
- Cover the fillets with a layer of onions; sprinkle with seasoning,
- Then a layer of potatoes; sprinkle with seasoning,
- Then a layer of tomatoes, season
- Alternate layers of onions potatoes and tomatoes
- Finish with tomatoes
- Cover and steam on high for 5 minutes,
- Then, carefully lift the lid, pour the lemon juice around the edges of the skillet,
- Cover again, cook on low for 20 - 25 minutes (check every 15 min; don't let dry)
- Dish is ready when the tomatoes and onions are fully cooked
- Serve
- ENJOY!

Jambalaya

YOU WILL NEED
- A 6-qt Dutch Oven
- 2 links of smoked sausage (pork, beef or a combo of pork/beef)
- 1 lb of chicken thighs (boneless/skinless)
- (OPTIONAL) One pork chop
- 1 Cup chopped onions etc.
- 1 tsp of Garlic and Parsley Salt
- 1 tsp of powdered/cubed chicken bouillon
- 2 Tbs of olive oil
- 1 8 oz package Jambalaya (Oak Grove makes a very good one)
- 1 qt of water

PREPARATION
- Cut up chicken to bite size pieces
- Slice sausage in ½ inch slices, then dice each slice into 4 pieces
- (OPTIONAL) Dice up the pork chop into ½ inch chunks
- PARBOIL the chicken in 1 qt of water with about 2 tsp of bouillon for 20 min. Drain the meat, place in a container. Save the broth in a separate container
- Dry the pan with a paper towel

COOKING
- Put the olive oil in the pan, set heat on "high"
- When the oil is hot add onions etc., with Parsley/Garlic Salt; sauté for about 3 minutes
- ADD all the meat; sauté 3 more minutes, until all the meat has been browned
- ADD the pack of Jambalaya; mix thoroughly
- SLOWLY add 2 Cups of the broth (per 8 oz mix)
- Cook very low for 20 - 25 minutes; at 20 minutes, NOT BEFORE, uncover and "fluff" the entire mixture. Cook another 3 - 5 minutes, until rice is done: fluffy and all the liquid has cooked off.
- Serve,
- ENJOY!

Macaroni and Cheese

YOU WILL NEED
- 2-qt saucepan
- 1 8 oz package of macaroni pasta
- 6 slices of American Cheese (See option below)
- ½ Cup milk OR Half and Half (this is VERY rich, AND yummy! but high on fat...)
- 1 tsp Garlic Parsley Salt, or Plain Salt (to your taste)
- 2 Tbs margarine

PREPARATION
- Prepare macaroni per directions (see directions under "Pasta")
- When "al dente" strain, discard water and hold macaroni in strainer
- Heat milk. This can be in microwave oven; set at "high" for 1 minute. Or heat on stove top for 2 minutes: DO NOT LET MILK BOIL. When done, hold milk in container.

COOKING
- Melt margarine in the 2-qt saucepan over medium heat
- Add macaroni and stir
- Sprinkle the Garlic and Parsley Salt (or plain salt) and thoroughly mix into the macaroni
- Lower heat to lowest setting and
- ADD cheese, stir and mix
- Slowly add and stir in the milk (or half and half)
- Keep stirring and mixing until all the cheese has melted
- Serve while still hot (OPTION: Lay 4 slices of American Cheese over the finished Macaroni – if your gang REALLY likes cheese! Let it melt over the hot pasta)
- ENJOY!

Mashed Potatoes

YOU WILL NEED
- 2-qt saucepan
- 4 – 6 white Russet potatoes
- 4 Cups water
- ½ tsp salt
- 1 tsp Garlic and Parsley Salt (add more or less to your taste)
- ¼ Cup margarine
- ½ Cup milk (half and half for richer potatoes)
- Long wooden spoon or potato masher

PREPARATION
- Peel and slice potatoes (slice into 4 or 6 pieces)
- Boil sliced potatoes in 4 Cups slightly salted water (1/2 tsp salt); boil for about 25 minutes

COOKING

(Potatoes are cooked when a fork slides easily into several of the boiling pieces)

NOTE: You can leave the potatoes in the hot water until you are about 15 minutes from serving the rest of your meal. If the water has cooled off, reheat it so the potatoes are nice and hot.

While the potatoes are cooking/reheating microwave or stovetop-heat the milk (DO NOT BOIL)
- When potatoes are done, pour out the water
- ADD the butter and the Garlic Parsley Salt
- Begin to break up the potatoes with the wooden spoon (that is, stir and mash the potatoes with the wooden spoon or potato masher)
- Gradually, ADD the heated milk, continue to stir and stir until potatoes are a smooth consistency
- Serve while still hot
- ENJOY!

Mashed Sweet Potatoes

YOU WILL NEED
- 2- qt saucepan
- 4 SWEET potatoes
- 4 Cup water
- ¼ Cup white OR brown sugar (add sugar to taste)
- ½ tsp powdered cinnamon (add to taste)
- ¼ Cup margarine
- ½ Cup milk (half and half for richer potatoes)
- Long wooden spoon or potato masher

PREPARATION
- Boil potatoes in 4 Cups water ; boil for about 25 minutes
- Potatoes are cooked when a fork slides easily into any of the potatoes.

COOKING
- While the potatoes are boiling, microwave or stovetop-heat the milk (DO NOT BOIL)
- When potatoes are done, pour out the hot water. Pour in cold water. Let cool for 2 minutes. Carefully, with a fork, take out each potato and remove the pealing. Place all the peeled potatoes back in the saucepan.
- ADD the butter,
- Begin to break up the potatoes with the wooden spoon (that is, stir and mash the potatoes with the wooden spoon or potato masher)
- Gradually, ADD the heated milk, sugar and cinnamon continue to stir and stir until potatoes are a smooth consistency
- Serve while still hot
- ENJOY!

Meat Sauce with Pasta

YOU WILL NEED
- 6-qt Dutch Oven
- 1 -2 lbs of ground beef (see meat section for other choices)
- Long wooden spoon
- 1 jar of Marinara sauce (see "Approved Cheating" section under Marinara Sauce)
- ½ to 1 Cup of chopped onions, etc
- 2 Bay Leaves
- 1 tsp of Garlic and Parsley Salt
- ½ tsp of Tony Chachere
- 1 Tbs of cooking oil or olive oil
- 1 8 oz can of tomato sauce (2 cans with 2 lbs of meat)
- OPTIONAL: for really tomatoey sauce, add a 15-oz can of diced OR crushed tomatoes
- 1 Tbs sugar
- ½ to ¾ pack of Spaghetti (see directions for Pasta)

PREPARATION
- Brown the meat (see section on "Basic Terms")
- Drain the grease (This is done by holding the lid over the pan with pot holders, leaving a slight slit, and tilting the pan until the grease literally drips out onto some container; discard the grease)
- Set the browned and drained meat aside

COOKING
- Using the same Dutch Oven, pour the cooking oil into it, set the burner on "high" when the oil is hot,
- Sauté the onions etc,
- Add Garlic Salt, Tony's and sauté for 1 - 2 minutes,
- Add the meat and stir, sauté for another 1 -2 minutes
- ADD the Marinara sauce, drop in the Bay Leaves, mix thoroughly
- Add can of tomato sauce (plus 1 can of plain water; OR here you can substitute the 15 oz can of sliced/chopped tomatoes), stir
- Adjust to taste, and ADD the sugar (the sugar cuts down on the acidity of the tomato)
- Cook the sauce covered for 30 minutes, stirring every 10 – 15 minutes
- When the sauce has 15 minutes to go,
- Prepare your pasta (see directions for pasta)
- When all is ready, serve meat sauce over pasta
- ENJOY!

Meatloaf*

YOU WILL NEED
- A Meatloaf Pan (you can buy a permanent one OR a throw-away aluminum foil one)
- 1 lb ground beef (ground sirloin preferably)
- ½ Cup of chopped onions, etc
- 1 Tbs Garlic and Parsley Salt (add more/less to taste)
- (OPTIONAL: ½ tsp Tony Chachere for spicy)
- 1 slice of bread, CRUMBLED
- 1/3 Cup Garlic Bread Crumbs (commercially packaged)
- 2 beaten eggs
- 1 8-oz can of tomato sauce (OPTIONAL: substitute 1 10-oz can Rotel for extra SPICY!)
- Preheat oven at 350 (i.e., set the oven to 350, and turn it on before you start preparations)

PREPARATION
- In a large bowl, combine all ingredients. This is best done by hand, which one of your children will love to do (Hey! If you don't have kids, it's kind of fun to get your hands right in there…. Talk about finger food!!!). Hold out about ¼ cu of tomato sauce
- Once all ingredients are thoroughly mixed, place in meatloaf pan, shaped to look like a loaf of bread,
- Spread the ¼ Cup of tomato sauce (or Rotel) over the top of the meatloaf with a spoon
- Cover the pan snuggly with aluminum foil

COOKING
- Bake at 350 degrees for 45 to 60 minutes
- When it is done, (it is done if there is little or no pink inside a test slice) slice and serve
- ENJOY!

*NOTE: You can go SIMPLE and get a McCormick "Meatloaf" seasoning pack and follow directions on the package (See "Approved Cheating" Section under "McCormick")

Pasta

There is a mystery about Pasta I have never been able to figure out: How much to measure for a specific number of servings you want. I usually cook half a pack of spaghetti for 2 or 3 servings, the whole pack for 4 or 5. Don't hold me to this. Experiment and be ready to store the excess...

There are 3 other mysteries, but I have a better handle on these;
1. How to tell when it's ready; what's "al dente", anyway?
2. How to keep it from clumping into one messy glump! And,
3. What PASTA? In this book pasta can be: spaghetti, linguini, fettuccine, rotini, penne pasta or egg noodles. However, unless otherwise specified, pasta is spaghetti. Yet, preparation is the same for all...

Let us proceed...

YOU WILL NEED
- A 6-qt Dutch Oven
- Pasta
- 1 qt of water (NOTE: 1 ½ qt of water for the whole pack)
- 1 tsp of salt (2 tsp for the whole pack)
- A strainer/colander
- 1 tsp of cooking oil (same amount for whole pack)
- 2 tsp of olive oil (or Canola oil if you prefer)
- Toothed pasta fork

COOKING
- Pour the water into your Dutch Oven
- Add the salt and the cooking oil (1 tsp)
- Heat water until it boils
- While it is boiling, with the burner remaining on "high",
- Carefully place the pasta into the boiling water. If cooking spaghetti it is best if you crack it in half
- Stir the pasta; make sure you separate and keep the pasta from clumping (Actually pick it up with the pasta fork and shake it over the water if it starts to clump...)
- KEEP BOILING
- Stir every 3 to 5 minutes with the pasta fork
- After 10 minutes of boiling and stirring, CAREFULLY remove ONE noodle with your pasta fork
- Taste/test the noodle. It may not be ready yet
- Taste/test in the same way UNTIL,
- Pasta is ready when your preference tells you it's cooked down the way you like it; that is, when it is pleasing to your teeth as you chew your "taste test" ("al dente", means "to the teeth": soft, chewy, but NEVER hard nor mushy!)
- Once it is ready, turn off the heat, and using pot holders, VERY CAREFULLY pour out the pasta onto your colander (which you have in your sink)
- While it is in the colander, pour in one tsp of olive oil, mix the pasta, then the other tsp of olive oil, again mix your pasta. This keeps it from "glumping"
- Your pasta is ready to use for your meal. NOTE: THE STRAINING AND MIXING IN YOUR COLANDER SHOULD BE YOUR LAST STEP BEFORE SERVING,
- ENJOY

Red Beans

YOU WILL NEED

- Red (kidney) beans, 1 lb.
- 6-qt. Dutch Oven
- 10-inch skillet
- Long wooden spoon
- ¾ Cup Chopped onions, etc.
- 1 tsp parsley/garlic salt (more or less to your taste)
- ½ tsp Tony Chachere's (optional: contains red pepper, black pepper and chilli pepper)
- 2 Bay leaves (optional, depends on your palate, but it does add flavor)
- 1 Tbs cooking oil
- ½ Tbs Margarine (optional, but tastes great!)
- 8 oz. can tomato sauce (optional)
- 2 – 3 links of smoked sausage (pork, or pork/beef)
- 1 qt. water
- 1 either SMOKED pork neck bone or SMOKED ham hock (for added flavor)
- A pot of rice (see directions for cooking rice)

PREPARATION

- Soak the pound of beans in your Dutch oven for 2 or more hours. Overnight will not harm them. HOWEVER, you do NOT HAVE TO soak them. Soaked beans take less time to cook.
- (1) Begin cooking your beans in a quart of water on "high" with the smoked pork neck bone. When it boils, reduce the heat until it is just bubbling gently and cover the pan. If it begins to spill out, lower the setting until it bubbles gently, covered. You want to have the beans bubbling, but not spilling over.
- NOTE: you will need to add water as it dries during the cooking stage. Add enough water, up to an inch above the beans and stir regularly. Each time you add water you have to again raise and lower heat until "bubbling without spilling". Continue,
- (2) Slice the sausage in 2 inch chunks; also, cut about half of one link in small, ¼ inch slices, set aside in holding container

COOKING

- Test the beans periodically after they have cooked about 45 minutes. Take one or two out with your wooden spoon and, once you've cooled them enough, bite and taste them. Once they are beginning to soften, proceed
- (3) Make your sauce: in the skillet, begin heating oil and margarine. Set burner on high. As soon as the margarine melts, add your onions etc. plus the spices you have selected from above. SAUTE'.
- After 3 minutes add the sausage you had cut up. Add the tomato sauce if you have selected to use it. Stir and sauté = for another 3 – 4 minutes.
- Carefully add this sauce to the beans.
- Prepare your rice,
- Cook beans for another 30 minutes covered. Stir every 15 min.; add water to keep soupy.
- Taste, taste, taste... add spices if it is lacking in flavor. This is the "taste and test" stage.
- When the flavor is right and the beans are soft, turn off your stove.
- Serve over rice
- ENJOY

Rice

THERE ARE AT LEAST 2 OR 3 DIFFERENT WAYS TO PREPARE RICE. YOU MAY FOLLOW THE DIRECTIONS ON THE PACKAGE, OR, THIS IS THE WAY I WAS TAUGHT, AND IT WORKS

ONE MAJOR CAUTION: THE WAY NOT TO BURN RICE IS TO WATCH IT AND TIME IT.

The proportions are a CONSTANT – 1 part rice, 2 parts water. Like, 1 ½ Cup rice, 3 Cups water; 2 cups rice, 4 cups water, etc. I will illustrate with 1 Cup of rice:

YOU WILL NEED
- A 2-qt saucepan with lid
- 1 Cup of LONG GRAIN white rice
- 2 Cups water
- ½ tsp salt
- 1 "dab" of margarine (about 1 ½ tsp); you can substitute oil for the margarine

PREPARE and COOK
- Pour in all ingredients into pan, stir
- Set burner on "high"
- AS SOON AS IT BOILS, stir and reset heat down to "medium high". (NOTE: If you are slow, and mixture spills over, remove pan from heat until it "simmers down" and burner adjusts to "medium high" setting. Put pan back on burner)
- Cook uncovered on "medium high" until almost all liquid cooks off, but is still "juicy" c. 5 minutes. NOTE: you must stay nearby or the rice will dry and burn, then
- Cover; reduce heat to LOWEST SETTING
- Time for 15 minutes with timer
- When timer "dings", uncover and "fluff" the rice with wooden spoon by stirring it from bottom to top. Put cover back on pan
- Cook an additional 3 to 5 minutes (AT LOWEST SETTING) until all liquid has dried. Turn burner off, leave covered
- Rice is ready to be served when the rest of the meal is ready.
- ENJOY!

Roast Chicken

YOU WILL NEED
- 1 Roasting Pan (with 2 inch sides). The usual dimensions are 9x13x2
- 1 long wooden spoon
- 1 THAWED Roasting or Frying Chicken (3 – 5 lb)
- 1 ½ Cups chopped onions etc.
- 2 ½ Tbs margarine
- 1 Tbs and 1 tsp Garlic and Parsley Salt
- OPTIONAL: for a little spice, 2 tsp Tony Chachere
- ½ Cup water

PREPARATION
- Preheat oven at 350 while preparing chicken
- Cut off the fat around the large opening at the tail
- Spread about a Cup of chopped onions on the bottom of the roasting pan, covering the whole surface,
- Sprinkle the onions with 1 Tbs Garlic and Parsley Salt, all along the bottom of the roasting pan,
- Do the same with 1 tsp Tony's
- Sprinkle the entire surface of the chicken with Parsley and Garlic Salt directly from the container
- Put ½ Cup of chopped onions inside the cavity of the chicken, move it around with the wooden spoon
- Also, sprinkle 1 tsp of Garlic and Parsley salt (and Tony's ?) inside the cavity of the chicken
- Scoop in ½ tsp of margarine inside the cavity
- Coat the breast and the thighs with the remaining 2 Tbs of butter (any margarine left over scoop onto the roasting pan
- Pour the ½ cup of water around the edge of the roasting pan

COOKING
- Place pan with chicken (breast up)in middle rack of preheated oven, set at 365 degrees
- Check after 1 hour.
- After the breast turns brown, turn the chicken over so that the back is up
- Cook 10 additional minutes or until back turns brown,
- Turn it over again so that the breast is up; cook another 10 minutes, then
- Check to see if done. Pierce the breast with knife point. Clear liquid should ooze out; if it is pink, cook for another 15 minutes. When you puncture it again and it oozes clear liquid, turn off the oven
- Take the pan out, carve all the pieces; use the sauce as gravy and serve,
- ENJOY!

Vegetables

There is nothing magical in this page EXCEPT this is the easy way to cook veggies... I have used this way to add side dishes to the meals I cooked when my girls were little. We managed to find a set of vegetables that became our regulars.

The "regulars", and by the way, you may find this method works for a lot of different frozen vegetables, (there might be some more popular than others around your table)... The usual culprits are – Peas, green beans, broccoli*, spinach**, lima beans+, black eye peas+, butter beans+, and corn

YOU WILL NEED
- A 2-qt sauce pan
- 1 to 2 Cups of water
- 1 to 2 tsp of chicken bouillon (1 per cup)
- A "dab" of butter
- 1 to 2 Cups of frozen vegetables

COOKING
NOTE: The water should be enough that it covers the veggies by 2 inches. Do not let it dry.

- Boil the water with the bullion
- ADD the vegetables and the butter
- Cook for 5 to 10 minutes at "low" setting, until the vegetables reach the chewiness that your crew likes; i.e., either firm or soft. Try not to let your motley crew insist on mushy as this cooks away the nutrients.
- That's it, no magic, just balanced meals...
- ENJOY

*The one exception is broccoli. The best way to cook broccoli is in a pan with 2 inches of water. Use a collapsible vegetable strainer inserted in your pan. Steam the broccoli (water is boiling) for about 5 minutes, covered. Remove from the burner and serve quickly. While this is the best way, they can be cooked as above. Just be careful as they get mushy real fast if cooked in water.

**I found that if I hard boiled one or two eggs and sliced them, then put the slices over the spinach, they would eat spinach! Give it a shot...

+Lima beans, black eye peas and butter beans taste great with precooked bacon bits added while they cook. (They also might need 15 or more minutes of cooking and more water)

Beef Vegetable Soup

YOU WILL NEED
- A 6-qt Dutch Oven
- 1 lb beef (stew beef; round steak OR sirloin cut up into bite-size cunks;)
- 6 to 8 cu water
- 3 carrots
- 1 stalk of celery
- 2 white potatoes
- 1 cu frozen "mixed vegetables"
- 2 Tbs cooking oil
- "dab" of margerine
- 1 tsp Garlic/Parsley Salt (OPTIONAL: ½ tsp of Tony Chachere's)
- 2 tsp chicken bouillon powder (or 2 cubes) NOTE: alternately, you may use tsp of beef bouillon (powder, or 2 beef cubes); or thirdly, 1 can of beef broth

PREPARATION
- Scrape carrot skin off with sharp edge of knife, cut off ends, then slice into ½ inch slices
- Peel and dice potatoes (Alterantely, slice potatoes in lengthwise, ¼ inch slices)
- Cut off ends of celery stalk, then slice into ¼ inch slices
- NOTE: if the mixed vegetables have vegies not to the liking of your "crew", any one or combination of other frozen vevies can be substituted (e.g. corn, peas, lima beans, lentils, green beans, black eye peas, etc.)

COOKING
- Saute chopped onions etc. in 2 Tbs of oil and margarine,
- ADD seasoning, saute' a total of 3, 4 minutes,
- ADD cut up beef chunks, saute' an additional 3 minutes, UNTIL beef has mixed with the sauteed oninions and seasoning and is browned, then
- STEAM mixture covered for about 1 to 2 minutes (i.e., cook at medium heat COVERED)
- Take off lid CAREFULLY (escaping steam can burn you), ADD all vegetables,
- STIR AND MIX thoroughly,
- ADD water and bouillon powder/cubes or broth
- Let boil for 5 minutes, ADJUST to taste; THEN cover and cook 30 minutes
- Serve with ladle into bowls
- ENJOY
-

About the Author

Lui Campos grew up in New Orleans. He obtained his Masters in Social Work degree at Louisiana State University. He began his marriage and family counseling practice in Baton Rouge, moved to New York where he expanded his specialties while living and practicing there for eight years.

When he and his wife returned to Baton Rouge, Louisiana, there were two beautiful daughters in tow who became his assistants in the Measuring Spoon Café the name they gave to the Sunday afternoon tradition of cooking their weekly meals after Campos became a single dad.

For additional recipes as well as other books by the author, go to:

www.themeasuringspooncafe.com

Made in the USA
Lexington, KY
15 December 2016